OLD BLUE

The Rarest Bird in the World

The publisher gratefully acknowledges the assistance
of the Literature Programme of the QEII Arts Council
in the publication of this book.

Dedicated to
the Chatham Islands Black Robin

Special thanks to Dr Don Merton,
Alison Davis and Brian Bell

Published by Ashton Scholastic, 1993

Ashton Scholastic Limited
Private Bag 92801, Auckland, New Zealand

Ashton Scholastic Pty Ltd
PO Box 579, Gosford, NSW 2250, Australia

Scholastic Inc.
730 Broadway, New York, NY 10003, USA

Scholastic Canada Ltd
123 Newkirk Road, Richmond Hill, Ontario L4C 3G5, Canada

Scholastic Publications Ltd
7-9 Pratt Street, London NW1 0AE, England

National Library of New Zealand
Cataloguing-in-Publication data

Taylor, Mary.
 Old Blue / by Mary Taylor ; [edited by Penny Scown].
Auckland, N.Z. : Ashton Scholastic, 1993.
  1 v.
  Picture story book for children.
  ISBN 1-86943-108-1
  1. Old Blue (Bird) 2. Black robin--Juvenile literature. 3. Rare birds--New
  Zealand. I. Scown, Penny. II. Title.
   598.0420993

9 8 7 6 5 4 3 2   3 4 5 6 7 8 9 / 9

Typesetting by Rennies Illustrations Ltd
Printed in Hong Kong

Far south, where the Pacific Ocean is cold and rough, there lies a group of lonely islands. Once they had no name. Then the Moriori people named them Rekohu. Today, these islands east of New Zealand are known as the Chatham Islands.

Long Ago

In the early world, forest scrambled over the islands. Strong winds battered the trees so they could not grow tall but they grew thick. Beneath their branches birds sang and raised their chicks.

Many different birds lived on the Chathams — in the bush, on the rocks, at the tops of the tallest trees, and even in burrows in the ground. Off shore, sea birds dipped into the ocean and circled on the wind. They nested on tall cliffs, while below them the sea crashed and seals gathered to rest and play.

In the bush lived hundreds of robins. Robins calling. Robins answering. Robins singing and darting through the trees. They looked much like robins elsewhere in the world, except that the Chatham robins were black. A soft, sooty black, with black beaks, black feet and sparkling big black eyes.

For thousands of years the birds lived here safely.

Then people arrived in boats. They built shelters near the sea where the seals lived. They caught fish and gathered forest plants. They killed some of the seals and birds, and ate birds' eggs. Sometimes a fire would spread from their camp into the forest.

Hundreds of years later, more people arrived. They killed thousands of seals for their skins, and hunted whales too. These settlers lit fires to burn down the forest. Then they brought animals to the islands. Where grass had grown over the broken, burnt ground, they released cows and sheep. Pigs pushed the tasty roots from the ground with tough snouts and trampled over the tiny seedlings which tried to begin a new forest. Further settlers brought possums who gobbled the tastiest berries, the new leaves and honey-sweet flowers.

But worst of all, the settlers brought carnivorous animals. When a robin hopped along the ground looking for grubs, a cat would suddenly spring from nowhere and pin down the little black bird with its sharp claws. When a robin returned to her nest, she would find broken eggs with the insides sucked clean. Nearby, a rat would lie curled up in its hole, fast asleep with a full belly. Sometimes a robin would return with a juicy meal for her chicks, but her chicks would be gone — inside the nest, just feathers and bones.

The Chatham Island birds backed away from the settlements. Back to the edges of the cliffs, and down to the steep banks where bush still flourished.

As more farmland replaced forest, more birds died. There were fewer places to live and nest; there was less to eat. The Chatham Island bellbird, swan, duck, fernbird, sea eagle and rail were never seen again.

The people who lived on the islands hardly noticed.

The Robins' Refuge

By 1900, there was only one island where the robins were safe. Little Mangere Island. It was too small, too steep and too dangerous for men and rats and cats.

The island's sheer cliffs were fringed with slippery kelp. All around, the sea swelled and broke into foam. On the top of the island grew tufts of scraggy trees. Vines curled like snakes around the trees, binding them tightly and choking them. Sunlight could no longer reach the ground. When the trees died, the wind whined and whistled as it snapped the bony branches. Scattered over the ground among the tree roots were burrows that belonged to mutton birds. The wind pushed itself in and out of the burrows and carried away the crumbly earth in clouds of dust.

This was a broken forest, a windy forest, a dying forest.

Spring 1970

High above the rocks, nestled in the branches of an ancient, broken tree, was a robins' nest. Although it was spring, the wind was still cold.

Beneath the female robin lay two warm eggs. When she felt a movement she stood and peeped under her snug feathers. A crack had appeared on one egg. Salty wind licked at the crack in the egg and blew sharply on the female's bent head. She lowered herself to protect the eggs. And there she stayed. Her mate arrived with a grub and pressed it into her beak. The two birds huddled together to pass the long, cold night.

In the grey dawn, a tiny head peeped out from under its mother. With a joyful twitter, the female cleared away the broken shell. The other egg never hatched.

As the days grew warmer there were more insects to catch. Taking turns, the robins fed their young one. The chick gobbled her food and grew strong. Soft, grey feathers began to grow over the chick's bald skin. From her nest she watched the world with alert black eyes.

Other robins watched the new chick. Sometimes they sang sad-sounding stories. Perhaps they sang about the death of their chicks. Or of eggs smashed by clumsy sea birds.

That summer, this was the only black robin chick to be raised in the whole world.

Twenty black robins sang in the summer light. For in all the world, there were only twenty black robins left to sing.

The Rarest Bird in the World

For some time before the chick was hatched, officers from the New Zealand Wildlife Service had been visiting the Chatham Islands to study and help the birds that lived there. They were concerned because the native birds had been gradually dying off. Some, they knew, had become extinct.

One summer, it was time to check Little Mangere Island. The chick was now one year old.

The wildlife officers climbed onto Little Mangere Island and searched for robins. The curious robins came close to watch. The men caught each robin and gently clipped a coloured band around one leg. They set them free again, naming each bird by the colour of its leg band.

One of the wildlife officers was Don Merton. When Don held the chick, he chose a blue leg band from his box. "You will be Blue," he whispered, as she flew from his hand.

Each spring the wildlife officers arrived at Little Mangere Island. At the end of each summer, they reported fewer and fewer robins. When Blue was almost six years old, they searched the entire island as usual but counted only *seven* black robins!

The robins were in trouble. Sometimes their eggs just didn't hatch. Sometimes the chicks died. Often there wasn't enough food. And each year more adult robins died.

Around them the forest was dying too. The robins were trapped on Little Mangere Island because their tiny wings were not strong enough to beat against the powerful winds that buffeted the island.

Don Merton's team discussed the situation.

"This is terrible!" said Don. "If we don't do something right now, there'll be no black robins left."

They decided that, above all else, the robins needed a new home. A new home with a thriving forest. Across a strip of deep water was a larger island with some shelter for bush birds — Mangere Island.

"We'll have to move them to Mangere Island," said Don. "But first we'll have to catch them, one by one."

So, between the trees the men draped a mist-net which reached from the highest branches to the ground. They threw plump grubs on the earth in front of the net. Don crouched in the bushes and whistled a robin-call. The robins listened. Then a robin with a red leg band spotted a wriggling grub and down he flew. A man rustled the bushes. Red panicked. He didn't see the net and flew straight into it, tangling his wings and claws.

Quickly Don untangled Red and carefully placed the small, frightened bird into a box with air holes. Inside the box was a perch and some leaves and grubs.

With the box strapped to his back, another man climbed down the steep and dangerous cliff to where a fisherman waited in a rubber dinghy. Together they left the island.

When Blue was caught in the net, her heart pounded. Gentle hands untangled her. Once inside the warm box she grew sleepy, and despite the strange bumping and noise, she tucked her head under her wing and slept.

One by one, all the robins were taken to Mangere Island.

When Blue was released on her new island home she flew to the highest tree and looked around. She saw large old trees. She saw strong young trees and bushes where she could hide. She saw places to nest, sunlight and shadow, leaves and seedlings on the forest floor. How she sang!

When the wildlife men scratched under the fallen leaves with their fingers, down flew the robins. On their old island, the dusty ground was full of burrows. But here there was a carpet of leaf litter. They soon learned that fat grubs lived under the leaves. Don found a weta and Blue appeared instantly beside him, snatching the insect from his hand. Here there was plenty to eat.

Confident that the robins were now safe in their new home, the men left the island. It was now up to the robins to settle down — to build nests and raise chicks.

Each year, Don and his team returned to check on the robins. But on their third visit they were horrified to count only *five* black robins! Five!

The black robin had become the rarest bird in the world. Only a miracle could save it from extinction.

By now, the newspapers of the world were printing stories about the Chatham Islands robin.

Old Blue

Of the five remaining robins only two were females. One wore a green band. Whenever Green laid eggs, they rarely hatched, and when they did, the chicks would die. Green tried and tried, but it was no good. She just couldn't breed successfully.

The other female was Blue. She was now nine years old, which is very old for a robin, as they usually live only four or five years. Like Green, she had not yet managed to raise any chicks. Robins usually stay with the same mate all their lives, but for some strange reason Old Blue suddenly decided to pair with a new mate — a young, sleek bird with a yellow leg band. Together they built a nest. Then Old Blue laid two eggs.

Each day the men watched with wonder. Wonder turned to excitement, excitement to hope. Was this the miracle they had been longing for? "It's almost as if she understands," they whispered to each other. "As if she knows."

Also on Mangere Island there lived busy little bush birds called warblers. Smaller than robins, warblers are brown-grey in plumage with white breasts and white eyebrows. The warblers were building nests. Nests of grass and moss bound with spiders' webs and lined with feathers.

By this time the men had decided on a new plan to help the robins. "We need foster parents," said Don. "Warblers might care for our baby robins, then the robins will be free to lay more eggs and together we'll produce twice as many chicks."

Don watched Old Blue's nest and waited until she had left the nest to feed. This was his chance.

He crept up to her nest and gently scooped out the first egg with a plastic spoon. Carefully, he placed it onto some cotton wool inside a jar. Then he scooped out the second egg.

Old Blue returned. She swooped down and landed abruptly on the edge of the nest. She peered inside. Nothing there. She looked all round the nest and underneath. No eggs. She looked amongst the leaves on the ground. No, the eggs hadn't fallen out. Puzzled, she flew over and landed on Don's shoulder. She peered through his glasses into his eyes.

"Don't worry, Old Blue," he whispered to her. "I'll look after those eggs. You lay some more." Old Blue flew off. No one saw her again that day.

Early next morning, Old Blue and Yellow were busy in another tree. They were starting a new nest.

This was exactly what Don had hoped for. He wanted Old Blue to lay more eggs than usual that summer. By taking her eggs, he was encouraging Old Blue to lay again. More eggs could mean more robins.

Don carefully carried one of Old Blue's eggs to a warbler's nest and waited until the warbler flew off. Into the nest he slipped a robin's egg. Just in time! Down flew the warbler. She wriggled into her nest and settled her warm feathers over the egg that was there. She didn't think it strange that an egg larger than her own had suddenly appeared.

Don found a second warbler's nest for Old Blue's other egg. Day after day, the warblers sat on Old Blue's eggs.

One morning Don heard cheeping from the first nest. Inside, he saw a tiny, damp chick. The warbler parents flew to and fro, feeding it with moths, insects and the occasional spider. Don's plan was working. The warblers had adopted the robin chick.

Old Blue's first chick was now ten days old. Don checked the nest that morning. Silence. He watched from the bushes. Time passed. A warbler perched some distance away, preening herself. No warblers arrived with food yet the chick was too young to leave the nest. What was going on?

Cautiously, Don peeped into the nest. There lay Old Blue's chick.   It was dead.   The warblers had left the nest because the young one had died.

The wildlife team gathered around the nest and looked at each other with sad, puzzled eyes. Why? Why had the precious robin chick died?

That evening they talked about Old Blue's chick. Gradually they realised what must have happened. Although the little warblers had worked hard all day, every day, fetching food for the chick, they hadn't chosen the right food for a robin. Old Blue would have fed her chick on grubs and wetas. The warblers had done their best. But it wasn't good enough. Old Blue's second chick must now be at risk.

Meanwhile, Old Blue had laid eggs in her second nest. Don carefully removed these eggs, too. Quickly, before Old Blue returned, he put something back into her empty nest. It was a nine-day-old chick. Her own chick, who until then had been raised by warblers.

When Old Blue returned she perched on a twig above her nest and cocked her head. She had just left a nest that held eggs too fresh to hatch. Now there were no eggs at all but a rather large chick sitting there. She whistled! The chick heard Old Blue and opened its beak. Old Blue was gone and back again in a flash. She pressed a fat grub into the baby's beak.

Green, the other robin female, was given one of Old Blue's eggs to hatch. A warbler was given the other.

"At least a warbler can incubate the egg," said Don. "As soon as the chick is hatched, we'll move it to a robins' nest."

Old Blue, Green, their mates, the warblers and the wildlife team worked hard until the end of summer. Together they raised four chicks.

Now there were nine black robins.

Next spring, the men returned to Mangere Island. They carried their heavy packs ashore, keen to find the robins.

Old Blue found them first. There she was, perched above their heads. She landed on Don's shoulder and peered through his glasses, deep into his eyes, chattering to him. She was old now but still her black eyes sparkled with excitement. Don whistled softly back to her. He loved this bird. There must always be black robins.

As soon as the men had settled into camp, Old Blue and Yellow began to chase each other through the trees. Then Old Blue perched on her favourite rock in the sun. Yellow returned with a grub which he fed to her.

Old Blue began her nest. She started at dawn and worked until dark while the other robins watched her. They also picked up moss in their beaks but didn't carry it anywhere. Instead, they continued to scratch the ground for grubs and doze in the spring sunshine.

By the time Old Blue had completed her first nest, the other robins were still pottering about.

Don removed her first two eggs. She built another nest and laid again. He took those eggs, too. She began a third nest . . .

That season, Old Blue laid a total of six eggs. She never knew what Don had done with the first four eggs she'd laid.

This time he had taken them to a large bushy island called South East Island in the hope that the tomtits who lived there would make better foster parents than warblers. Tomtits are bigger than warblers. They look rather like robins, with pointed beaks and bright eyes, but they have yellow chests. Broody tomtit females are fat and fluffy.

Don slipped Old Blue's eggs into tomtit nests. When the tomtits returned they just sat on whatever was there, fluffed out their feathers and chattered to Don from their snug nests. "You love sitting on eggs, don't you," he whispered to them. "You think of nothing else but eggs. You're wonderful parents for robins."

The robin chicks grew fat in the tomtits' nests.

Just before they were ready to fledge, Don collected the young robins. He took them back to Mangere Island, two hours away by sea, where he placed them in robins' nests so that they would learn to be black robins.

Meanwhile, Old Blue had been sitting on her third batch of eggs.

As Don walked by one morning, Old Blue stood up in the nest. There were two new chicks.

As soon as she flew off to find food, Don opened his brooder-box. He lifted out three of the South East Island chicks and lowered them into Old Blue's nest.

When Old Blue returned she saw *five* hungry beaks wide open in the nest. There had been only two when she'd left! She scratched her head with her claw and off she flew.

She dived on a cockroach. She hauled on a weta. Then back to the nest she flew and pushed food into the nearest open mouth. She called to Yellow.

Old Blue and Yellow worked all day to feed their large family.

Each day Don helped. He would stop at the nest to offer mealworms and juicy grubs from his jar. Once Old Blue arrived with a grub but found her chicks were so full that their beaks had clamped shut. Old Blue cocked her head to peer at Don and then gulped down the grub herself. Don held up a bug from his jar. She gobbled that too, her black eyes twinkling at Don's smiling face.

By the end of that summer the black robins numbered twelve.

The following spring, Old Blue's sons and daughters were breeding. Her grandsons and granddaughters were also breeding. There were more black robins than there had been for years. And all turned out just like Old Blue. They were strong, and they worked hard all spring and summer to raise their chicks.

When the first cold southerly hit Mangere Island and tore leaves from the trees, it was time for the men to return once more to New Zealand. They left behind them nineteen black robins.

Don was the last to leave the island. As he had done each year before leaving, he looked out for Old Blue. At the side of the track he spotted her standing on her favourite rock warming herself in the last of the summer sunlight. She turned a little as Don whispered his thanks, then she tucked her head under her wing. Her feathers were in tatters and she looked very tired.

Another winter passed. When the wildlife team arrived the following October they found all the robins except Old Blue. Newspapers throughout the world printed the headlines:

Famous robin Old Blue presumed dead

An Exceptional Bird

Old Blue, the miracle bird, had lived over thirteen years, a remarkable age for a robin. No other robin has ever lived anywhere near that age. And when there seemed to be no hope for the Chatham Island Black Robin to survive as a species, Old Blue suddenly changed her mate and tried to breed just one more time. She tolerated the endless manipulation of her nests by people. She laid more eggs than any other black robin and mothered more chicks.

Old Blue and Yellow are the great ancestors of every black robin alive today. Without them, the Chatham Island Black Robin would simply be another name on the long list of birds and animals lost forever.

For five more years the wildlife people used tomtits to help the robins raise chicks. By 1989 the number of robins had increased to over a hundred. Don Merton and his colleagues decided that cross-fostering could now stop. Robins could be left to breed on their own.

Today there is a robin population living on Mangere Island and another population on South East Island, a total of about 130 birds. One day, black robins may be introduced to selected reserves on Pitt Island as well.

Saving the black robin was a true team effort involving wildlife officers, volunteers, local Pitt Islanders and the Chatham Islands community, and of course the birds — the warblers, the tits and the robins.

This is the story of hard work and miracles, and of people who cared enough to help save a little black bird on a group of lonely south-sea islands.

The Plaque

This plaque was placed at the Chatham Islands Airport in November 1991. It is to honour the life of Old Blue and the years of work to save the Black Robin species.

Photo by: RAEWYN EMPSON

Don Merton

New Zealander Dr Don Merton is one of the world's most outstanding managers of endangered species.

An officer with the New Zealand Department of Conservation (formerly Wildlife Service), birds have always fascinated him. As a small boy he would bring home wild goldfinch chicks for his grandmother's canary to raise — a simple cross-fostering experiment which he applied years later to save the world's rarest bird.

A practical, innovative and positive person who does not give up once he has set himself goals, Don has managed many wildlife projects in his home country and elsewhere in the world. At present he is leading the project to save the world's heaviest parrot, the rare New Zealand kakapo.

To the children who read this book, Don says "The future care of species will fall into the hands of you who are today's young people. Tomorrow, you must take care of them."

Illustrated Birds of the Chatham Islands

Degree of Vulnerability   *Rare → threatened → endangered → extinct*

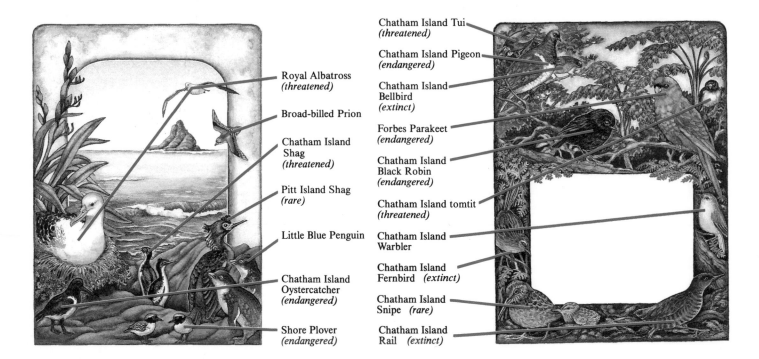

Royal Albatross *(threatened)*

Broad-billed Prion

Chatham Island Shag *(threatened)*

Pitt Island Shag *(rare)*

Little Blue Penguin

Chatham Island Oystercatcher *(endangered)*

Shore Plover *(endangered)*

Chatham Island Tui *(threatened)*

Chatham Island Pigeon *(endangered)*

Chatham Island Bellbird *(extinct)*

Forbes Parakeet *(endangered)*

Chatham Island Black Robin *(endangered)*

Chatham Island tomtit *(threatened)*

Chatham Island Warbler

Chatham Island Fernbird *(extinct)*

Chatham Island Snipe *(rare)*

Chatham Island Rail *(extinct)*